PowerKiDS
Readers
Happy Holidays!

Hanukkah

Josie Keogh

PowerKiDS
press.

New York

Published in 2013 by The Rosen Publishing Group, Inc.
29 East 21st Street, New York, NY 10010

First Edition

Editor: Amelie von Zumbusch
Book Design: Andrew Povolny

Photo Credits: Cover Tome Le Goff/Photodisc/Getty Images; p. 5 Pam Ostrow/Photolibrary/Getty Images; p. 7 iStockphoto/Thinkstock; p. 9 Michael Cogliantry/Photodisc/Getty Images; p. 11 Hemera/Thinkstock; p. 13 © iStockphoto.com/Sarah Bossert; p. 15 © iStockphoto.com/Sean Locke; p. 17 Jupiterimages/Photos.com/Thinkstock; p. 19 Fuse/Getty Images; p. 21 Jupiterimages/Photos.com/Thinkstock; p. 23 Katrina Wittkamp/Photodisc/Getty Images.

Library of Congress Cataloging-in-Publication Data
Keogh, Josie.
 Hanukkah / by Josie Keogh. — 1st ed.
    p. cm. — (PowerKids readers: happy holidays!)
Includes index.
ISBN 978-1-4488-9626-4 (library binding) — ISBN 978-1-4488-9708-7 (pbk.) —
ISBN 978-1-4488-9709-4 (6-pack)
1. Hanukkah—Juvenile literature. I. Title.
BM695.H3K46 2013
394.267—dc23
                                    2012020040

Manufactured in the United States of America

CPSIA Compliance Information: Batch #W13PK3: For Further Information contact Rosen Publishing, New York, New York at 1-800-237-9932

Contents

Hanukkah lasts eight days.

It honors what took place in the Jewish Temple.

The oil lasted for eight nights!

That is why you eat foods
fried in oil.

Latkes are made of potatoes.

13

Light the **menorah**!

The **shamash** is in the middle of it.

There are gifts.

Spin the dreidel!

20

21

You can win gelt.

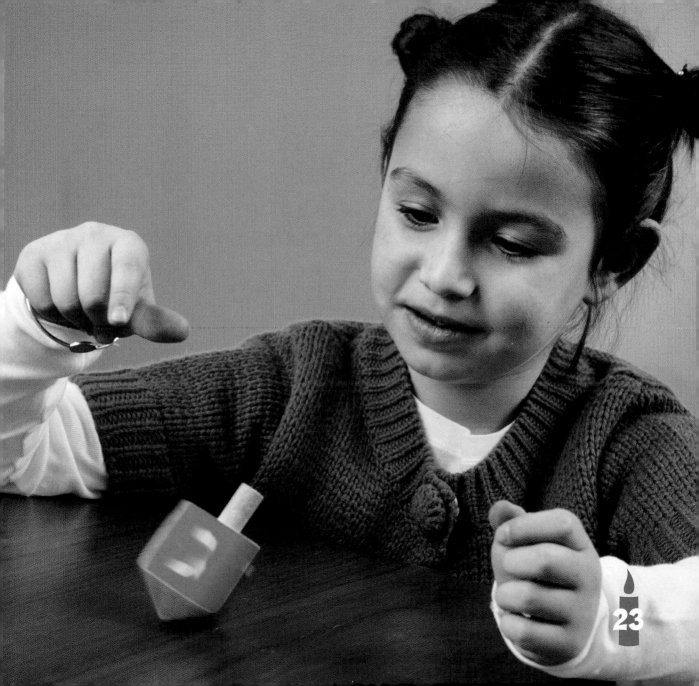

WORDS TO KNOW

latke

menorah

shamash

INDEX

WEBSITES

Due to the changing nature of Internet links, PowerKids Press has developed an online list of websites related to the subject of this book. This site is updated regularly. Please use this link to access the list:

www.powerkidslinks.com/pkrhh/hanuk/